FIGHTING PATROL TRAINING

by

COL. G. A. WADE M.C.

The Naval & Military Press Ltd

Published by the
The Naval & Military Press
in association with the Royal Armouries

Unit 10 Ridgewood Industrial Park,
Uckfield, East Sussex, TN22 5QE
Tel: +44 (0) 1825 749494
Fax: +44 (0) 1825 765701

MILITARY HISTORY AT YOUR FINGERTIPS
www.naval-military-press.com

ONLINE GENEALOGY RESEARCH
www.military-genealogy.com

ONLINE MILITARY CARTOGRAPHY
www.militarymaproom.com

The Library & Archives Department at the Royal Armouries Museum, Leeds, specialises in the history and development of armour and weapons from earliest times to the present day. Material relating to the development of artillery and modern fortifications is held at the Royal Armouries Museum, Fort Nelson.

For further information contact:
Royal Armouries Museum, Library, Armouries Drive,
Leeds, West Yorkshire LS10 1LT
Royal Armouries, Library, Fort Nelson, Down End Road, Fareham PO17 6AN

Or visit the Museum's website at
www.armouries.org.uk

In reprinting in facsimile from the original, any imperfections are inevitably reproduced and the quality may fall short of modern type and cartographic standards.

be straggled all over the place. Make up your mind inflexibly that except for the scouts you are going to keep all your men in a compact body so that you can use them all together to hit the enemy a strong, forceful and heavy blow.

The SECOND great failing is that the patrol LOSES ITS MOMENTUM. It sets off in great style, full of fire and fury. Then a distant shot is heard and immediately everyone in the patrol starts creeping, crawling, taking cover and returning the fire. This is just what the Germans want: they can take careful, steady aim, they can pick the patrol off one by one, they can carry out their plans unhindered, and they feel on TOP.

But how different their feelings when they open fire on a patrol which, instead of faltering or hesitating, shows determination to come to grips, a patrol which firmly and resolutely carries out a dashing attack, every man knowing exactly what is required of him!

Then the Germans' fire becomes wild and inaccurate. They begin to think about their retreat. They glance with fear at the glinting bayonets which begin to converge. Their stomachs turn to ice. They sense the deadly determination of the approaching patrol, and before they know it, without any orders from their brains, their legs are running like hell.

This concludes my sketch outline of fighting patrols. You have the framework: let your own exercise and experience fill in the gaps.

And then, when the Great Moment comes for you to lead your fighting patrol against the invading Huns KEEP YOUR MEN TOGETHER, KEEP UP YOUR MOMENTUM, and you will find yourself enjoying the FINEST SPORT ON EARTH!

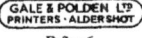

P 8996

SUMMARY

TRAINING.

>Attractive—popular.
>Much can be done indoors.
>**Open air**—tactical features.
>Useful information when invader comes.

SIX CHARACTERISTICS

>Determination—Skill—Ability.
>Instinctive reaction—Simple movements—Confidence.

DETERMINATION TO ATTACK.

>Get the right idea.
>"Spoiling for a fight."
>Safety achieved only by **killing the enemy.**
>Safer to **attack** than be **attacked.**
>Initiative always has advantage.

SKILL IN HANDLING WEAPONS.

>Shooting in darkness.
>Bayonet fighting in dark room.
>Fire control important—not much S.A.A.
>Care when using grenades.

ABILITY TO MOVE PROPERLY.

>Straggling—careless exposure.
>Every man should see how patrol looks.
>Study of ground—imitation of natural features.
>Cows.
>Small proportion always watching others.

INSTINCTIVE REACTION TO ATTACK.

>Attack and defence drills often.
>At unexpected times.
>Loud shouting—shed artificial restraint.
>Quick movement—intense stillness.
>Sudden attacks—no orders.
>**One reaction—hit back hard.**

SYNCHRONIZATION.

> Wonderful practice possibilities.
> Vital importance.
> Avoidance of casualties.
> Well-timed pincer movements.
> Charging at fifty yards.

CONFIDENCE.

> Comes with **practice**.
> Study ground **before** exercise.
> Leader must study.
> Men sense knowledge.

STREET FIGHTING.

> Definite objective.
> Covering fire.
> Best attack from yards and gardens.
> Keep to the **right**.
> Scouts.
> Snipers.
> Movements **quick** across open—**deliberate** in cover.

HOW TO CLEAR HOUSES (Plate 1).

> **As in Attack Drill.**
> Covering fire.

FIGHTING PATROL COMPETITIONS.

> Every team same task.
>
> | | |
> |---|---|
> | Shooting | 10 |
> | Grenade throwing | 5 |
> | Action of Patrol:— | |
> | Plan | 12 |
> | Speed | 20 |
> | Ground and cover | 20 |
> | Precautions | 9 |
> | Action at objective | 10 |
> | General | 14 |
> | | 100 |
>
> Prize for criticism.

EXAMPLE OF FIGHTING PATROL EXERCISE (Plate 2).

Stress **look-out** at **all times.**

OBSERVATIONS ON ANOTHER EXERCISE (Plate 3).

Start steadily—work up in a crescendo.
Final **swoop** on to enemy.
Loss of purposefulness.
Two Fallacies.
 "Compact body vulnerable."
 "Compact body conspicuous."
"Machine gun here—whole party wiped out."
Makes a machine gunner laugh!
Parties never wiped out at close range.
Best, quickest, **safest** way compact body.

Second Fallacy.

Crossing open spaces in hedges.
Compact mass hard to see.
Danger of rhythmic movement.

A WELL-PLANNED FIGHTING PATROL ACTION

(Plate 4).
Road to CALDOS.

TWO FINAL HINTS.

1. Do not **dissipate your force.**
 Fighting patrol versus fifteen Germans.
 Easy meat **if patrol** keeps together.
 Danger of splitting into sections.
 Everything conspires to spread the men out.
 "**Strong, heavy, forceful** blow!"

2. Do not **lose momentum.**
 One shot makes them crawl.
 Just what Germans want.
 Converging bayonets.
 "Legs running like hell."

THE GREAT MOMENT.

Keep your men together.
Keep up your momentum.
You will find yourself enjoying the finest sport on earth!

FIGHTING PATROL TRAINING

I

THE SIX ESSENTIALS

HAVING formed in our minds a complete picture of the fighting patrol's activities in war, and having realized its immense value both in attack and defence, you will naturally be keenly interested to know what form of training will most quickly produce fighting patrols of such a standard that they can unhesitatingly engage ANY enemy, without doubt as to the result.

Fortunately, if carefully thought out, training for fighting patrols can be made exceedingly attractive and popular; which is the great essential for rapid progress.

A surprising amount of training can be done indoors on wet days and nights, but every possible moment should see the fighting patrol operating over the countryside because that is where it will have to "do its stuff," and during training the patrol will be acquiring knowledge of the tactical features which may be invaluable when the invaders materialize.

There are SIX principal characteristics we should aim to produce in our fighting patrols:—

(1) **Determination** to attack any enemy quickly and bloodthirstily.

(2) **Skill** in handling of weapons.

(3) **Ability** to move quietly, inconspicuously and *quickly* across the landscape.

(4) **Instinctive reaction** to attack.

(5) **Power** to carry out simple, well-synchronized pincer and other movements.

(6) **Confidence** in their Patrol and Section Leaders.

I now propose to take each of these characteristics separately.

II

DETERMINATION TO ATTACK

In all training there is nothing so effective as getting the right idea from the very commencement, and, from the first moment, it should be instilled into the members of the fighting patrol that their job is to FIGHT.

They go out LOOKING for a FIGHT!

They are SPOILING for a fight. Their one idea is to GO FOR THE ENEMY on sight, and this should be rubbed in frequently during training, especially if signs of hesitancy appear in movements and operations.

Periodic lectures should be given on what a German victory would mean to this country, with lists of authentic atrocities from occupied countries, and their implied threat to the men's own loved ones.

Then should be given illustrations of the advantage the ATTACK always enjoys.

In other words, men must be taught that in the LONG view their safety can only be achieved by KILLING THE ENEMY and in the SHORT view it is far safer to *attack* than be *attacked*. The INITIATIVE has the advantage every time.

III

SKILL IN HANDLING WEAPONS

The better the patrol can shoot the more effective it will be against an enemy, and in addition to ordinary musketry time should be spent practising the men in shooting at targets lost in the darkness but rigged up to make sounds or to emit a very dim glow. This teaches them to fire by the feel of their rifles.

A dark room fixed up with bayonet-fighting dummies which produce faint sounds is grand sport, but send only one man in at a time and see that the operator of the sounds is absolutely safe or the practice may become slightly too realistic.

Fire control is also a very important subject because the sections may have to cover each other's retirement over a considerable stretch of country, and members of a fighting patrol do not normally take out a large supply of S.A.A.

A good tommy-gun or L.M.G. artist is very valuable to a patrol, and bombing should be practised assiduously. Make it interesting by contests in throwing bombs into upstairs windows, and over walls, etc., on to invisible targets.

In all these practices insist on the thrower always taking precautions against being " hoist with his own petard."

Incidentally, it is no use thinking that if you lie down in the open you are safe from a Mills " petard " you have thrown. You will always need some cover, no matter how far you can throw.

Be sure to organize some throwing of dummy bombs at " sound " targets lost in darkness.

Careful study should be devoted to selection of sites from which to give covering fire for attack, and also for withdrawal.

IV

ABILITY TO MOVE PROPERLY

This requires continual practice, but it is never boring if, before setting out, every man is told precisely what faults to look out for (straggling, careless exposure, etc.), and interest is doubled if each man is given the opportunity of seeing how the rest of his patrol looks when moving at distances from one hundred yards up to two miles away.

Before setting out the patrol should be invited to study the ground to be traversed, and should be practised in imitating various natural features: for instance, if there are some clusters of gorse to be passed the patrol should be halted there and sections should be ordered to " freeze " into shapes resembling a gorse cluster as closely as possible. Each section should see the others' imitations, and efforts to simulate sitting cows, etc., give rise to merriment and implant the right idea.

Practise crossing gaps, avoiding rhythmic movement; use of shadow side of walls, hedges, woods, etc.

Do not forget always to have a small proportion of the patrol WATCHING how the others perform.

V

INSTINCTIVE REACTION TO ATTACK

The attack and defence drills detailed in my previous lecture should be carried out frequently, particularly at unexpected times. In the attack drill the men should be encouraged to yell as loudly as they can, for nothing more thoroughly arouses the martial spirit. Once a man has shouted at the very top of his voice he has shed the artificial restraint of years and is well on the way to becoming the sort of savage warrior we want.

In the defence drill the sudden transition from quick movement to intense stillness is excellent discipline, and great importance should be attached to this; in fact, men should be specially detailed to watch for even the flicker of an eyelid. The periods of absolute stillness should be gradually extended.

Sudden attacks should be staged upon the patrol and occasionally no orders to meet it should be issued by the Leader. This will soon prove if the patrol has the right idea of instinctive reaction.

A fighting patrol should have only ONE reaction to attack—TO HIT BACK, INSTANTLY and HARD.

The enemy will soon learn that our fighting patrols are good things to keep away from.

VI

IMPORTANCE OF SYNCHRONIZATION

No aspect of fighting-patrol training holds greater possibilities for entertaining and instructive exercises than practising synchronized movements.

The vital importance of perfect timing by attacking sections in preventing casualties should be drummed in time after time until every member of the patrol fully appreciates the relationship between accurately timed movements and his own safety.

The risks a patrol runs of the enemy taking it section by section should be clearly illustrated by examples worked out on the ground. For contrast should be demonstrated a deadly, well-timed, pincer movement by two sections covered by fire from the other section.

Exercises in which an objective is indicated and sections are told to approach to within fifty yards by different routes and then charge home at a given signal will soon illustrate the point.

Later on distances should be increased and more difficult ground chosen, but the men should not actually charge for more than fifty yards.

VII

CONFIDENCE

Confidence will come with practice. To begin with, the Patrol Leader should very carefully go over the ground before the patrol is taken out. He must know what he wants, and all orders and instructions should invariably be given through him.

If the Leader studies fighting patrols until he knows his subject thoroughly the men will sense this and feel confident that they are being well led.

VIII

TACTICS—STREET FIGHTING

The fighting patrol may at any time have to "do its stuff" in a town or village, so it should be trained in the underlying principles of street fighting:—

(1) The patrol should set itself a definite objective to clear.

(2) No one should advance towards the houses to be attacked until men detailed to provide covering fire are in position.

(3) Usually houses are better attacked from the yards and gardens at the back, rather than up the street.

(4) If the patrol has to advance up the street it should keep to the right. This means that the enemy in order to shoot has to lean well out of the windows and so is a better target for our covering fire.

(5) The patrol should have scouts out to guard against surprise, and also the rear should be covered.

(6) Marksmen should be placed on any dominant feature so as to pick off the enemy retreating or prevent hostile reinforcements arriving.

(7) Movements should be at the double across open spaces and deliberate when there is cover.

Fighting Patrol Clearing Houses

In accordance with attack drill, No. 2 Section attacks on the right. Three men take up position at A while remainder of section tackles houses at B.

Similar action is taken on the left by No. 3 Section.

Object of men at A is threefold: (1) to give covering fire to remainder of section; (2) to "bump off" any enemy bolting across C; and (3) to prevent reinforcements crossing road to assistance of enemy at B. No. 1 Section gives covering fire along the street and watches rear of Nos. 2 and 3 Sections. It is also available as a reserve.

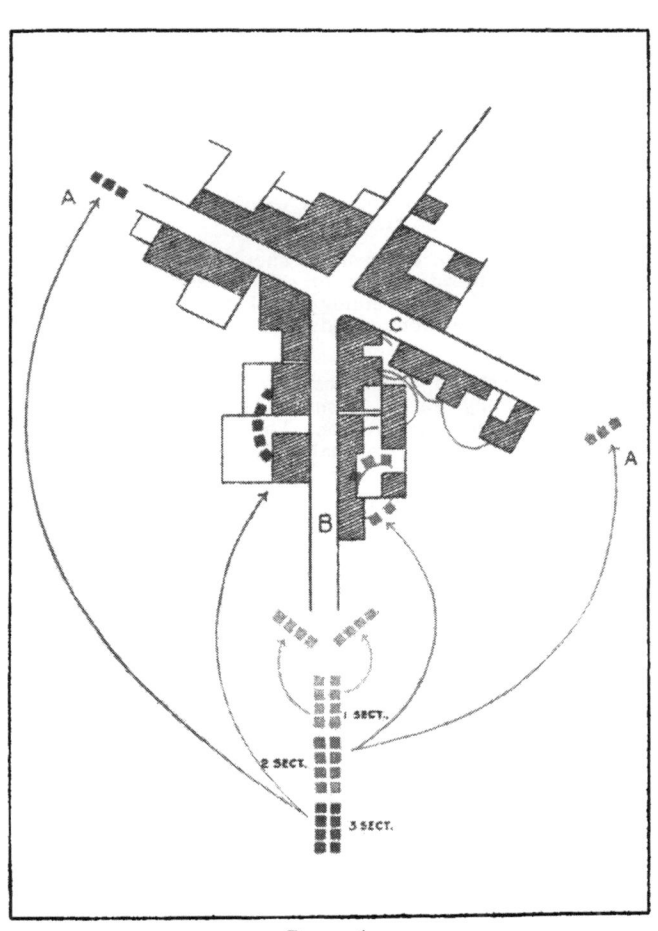

PLATE 1
FIGHTING PATROL CLEARING HOUSES

IX

FIGHTING PATROL COMPETITIONS

A splendid way of exciting and maintaining interest is to stage Fighting Patrol Competitions. Every effort should be made to encourage the men to watch these contests, as they are most instructive. Each competing team is given exactly the same task, and the different ways in which they tackle it bring out many points.

This is how the competition should be run. First get some well-disposed person to offer a cup for the Best Fighting Patrol. The winning patrol should be allowed to hold this for two months and then another contest should be held.

The competition should be divided into three parts: Part 1, Shooting; Part 2, Dummy Grenade Throwing; and Part 3, Fighting Patrol Action. The last is, of course, the important part, and a reasonable allotment of marks is as follows:—

SHOOTING	10
DUMMY GRENADE THROWING	5
ACTION OF FIGHTING PATROL—	
Plan	12
Speed	20
Use of ground and cover	20
Precautions against surprise	9
Action on reaching objective	10
General (issue of orders, turn-out, etc.)	14
Total	100

Competitors who have not yet taken part should not be allowed to see the exercise. There should be one umpire with the patrol and one with the enemy.

A very good idea is to offer a prize to the spectator who sends in the best criticism of the competition within a week of the contest. Forms for entry should be distributed on the spot.

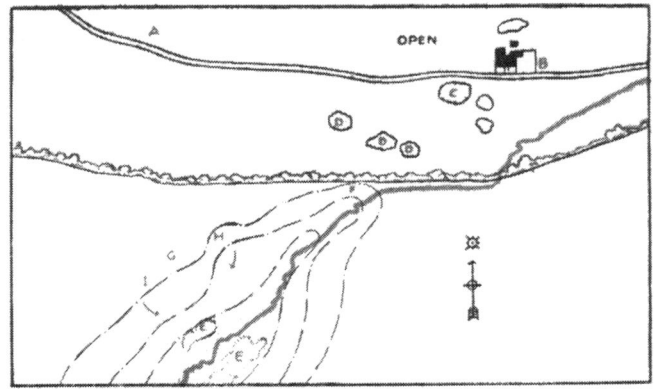

PLATE 2

Example of Fighting Patrol Exercise

Patrol was ordered to cover road from A to B in search of enemy. Four enemy were concealed in gorse at C with orders to let scouts go by and fire on the main body of the patrol at close range. Main body of enemy (about a dozen) were concealed in bracken at E with orders to move immediately firing was heard, proceed down the valley stealthily and attack the patrol.

The objects of this exercise were to stress the importance of scouts doing their work thoroughly, and to demonstrate the absolute necessity of a look-out in *all directions* at *all times*.

What actually happened with most patrols was that immediately shots were fired from C the Leader and *everyone else* took cover behind bushes at D and became so intent on attacking the enemy at C that they were oblivious of everything else and the remaining enemy just quietly strolled down the valley and shot them in the back at close range through the hedge F.

In one case, however, the scouts were well out on the flank and one walked straight into the enemy at C. He was pulled down in a second, but the rear scout had spotted what had happened and signalled back. The Patrol Leader placed covering fire at G (completely dominating the enemy at E), while the two other sections charged down from H and I and scuppered the lot.

The following are some observations made upon another competition. Each patrol started from the road, where it was told that a small party of German paratroops had dropped near the station and was busy preparing the bridge at Y for demolition. Patrol was ordered to proceed there at once to attack the enemy and if possible to save the bridge.

The obvious course of action was to push out scouts along the stream and on both flanks as shown by phantom line and then for the patrol to proceed along the bed of the stream by bounds as indicated to Z Farm.

Here No. 1 Section should give covering fire while the other two sections deliver a pincer attack on the bridge and station.

Certain weaknesses were obvious in all the patrols, but varying in degree.

Upon receiving instructions from the umpire the Leader should have spent a minute or so in careful scrutiny of the ground, looking out for obstacles and potential dangers and selecting the best line of approach to the objective, etc.

Then he should have called his Section Leaders and explained everything fully to them so that the information could be passed to the men. Precious though time is, a little spent in this manner at the beginning would have amply repaid.

All the patrols set off in great style, but tended to lose their purposefulness as they neared their objective. This, of course, is entirely the wrong way round. They should have started steadily and worked up in a crescendo (*i.e.*, to the final swoop on to the enemy).

This loss of purposefulness was due to dispersion of the patrol and immediately became marked after the wood was encountered; in fact, in one or two cases the Leader never regained control. Consequently, when the patrols got to within hitting distance of the enemy they faltered, then filtered up bit by bit, waited, hesitated, and finally delivered an unco-ordinated assault which would have cost them a lot of casualties.

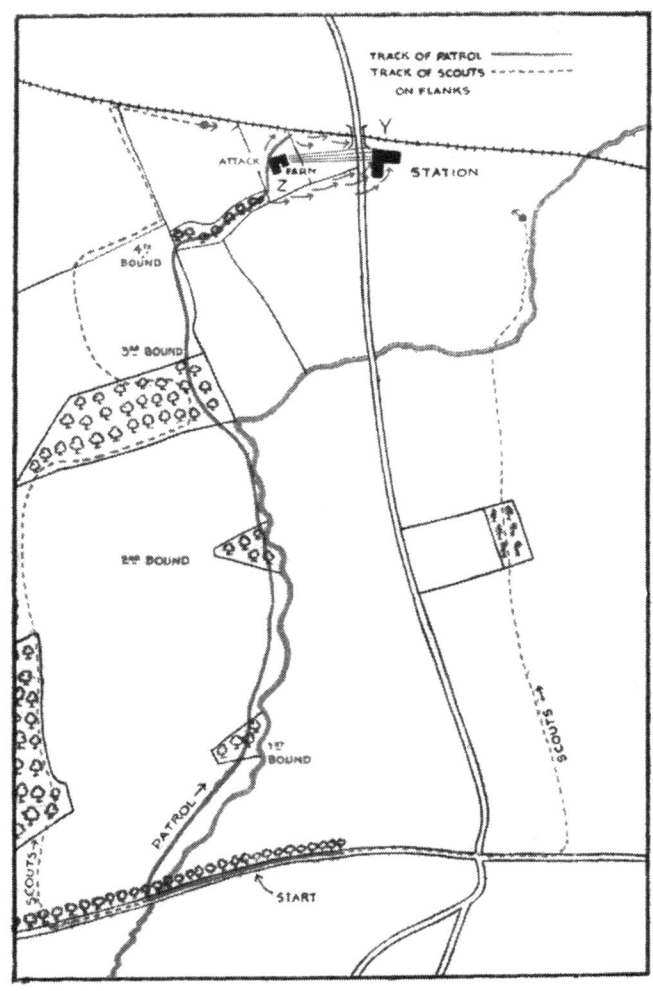

PLATE 3

Now this dispersion appeared to be brought about by a belief that (1) a compact body would be wiped out by machine-gun fire; (2) a compact body would be more conspicuous.

Both these ideas are FALLACIES.

Take (1). How often we hear people say, "There is a machine gun here, so the whole party would have been wiped out."

That usually seems to settle it; but it makes a machine gunner laugh!

During over three years' fighting as machine gunners there were a number of occasions when we found compact bodies of the enemy advancing at close range—targets we had been dreaming of during months of squalor. Coldly and deliberately we let them come on and when we finally opened fire it looked like certain wholesale slaughter.

But what was ALWAYS the case?

The instant we opened up on them the party flung themselves on the ground and took advantage of any bit of cover within reach. Later on when we went down to inspect the " bag " there would be only a couple of dead and three or four wounded. The rest of the twenty or thirty who had made such a glorious target and who had received our deadly concentrated fire had simply vanished (to fight somewhere else!).

NEVER have I seen a case where, with every advantage, a machine gun has succeeded in anywhere near annihilating a party of the enemy at very close range.

Now if the above incidents happened with MACHINE GUNS on unemotional tripods the lesson applies with double force to light machine guns, which nearly always fire high when the gunner is under nervous strain.

Whenever I see automatic weapons my heart rejoices; but I cherish no illusions about their potentialities, for bitter experience has taught me that the time factor nearly always robs them of the bulk of their possible victims. Consequently, if the patrol is covered by a good screen of scouts and is trained to flatten instantly if fired upon, the best, quickest AND SAFEST way to progress is in a close, compact body, steady, deadly, purposeful, eager and intent —like a beast of prey ready to swoop on to the enemy. ALL aimless dispersion and wandering must be cut out rigorously.

Now for the second fallacy. In this kind of country the advance of the patrol will be largely along the hedges, and these have periodic open spaces which the patrol must cross, if possible without attracting the enemy's attention. If the patrol is bunched up tight and led across it is quite difficult to spot from any distance, as it looks so like the hedge. Only its movement gives it away, so it should move slowly and evenly.

In the competition the dispersed patrols passed gaps, individual after individual, giving an intermittent rhythmic movement which absolutely drew the eye towards it from a mile away.

The attacks at the end were unconvincing and lacked just the very thing the fighting patrol should have—DASH.

The Leaders should have made a simple plan (the simpler the better), such as a pincer movement or a party sent to create a diversion while the main body RUSHED the enemy's position.

I never heard a man yell as he charged, whereas the whole lot at the end should have been roaring like fiends from hell as they closed with the enemy.

Here is an example of a well-planned fighting patrol action (see Plate 4, page 18):—

Enemy air activity had been pronounced for some hours and news had been received that paratroops had been dropped a few miles away, so a fighting patrol was sent to patrol the road to CALDOS.

When a scout arrived at A he found a wounded man who said that about fifteen enemy paratroops had landed on the football field, had placed out a landing sign, and proceeded up to a large rock on the top of the hill.

The scout immediately fetched the Patrol Leader, but the man was dead, so no further information was forthcoming.

The Leader then summed up the situation as follows:—

(*a*) The enemy had put out a landing sign, so more Huns could be expected at any moment.

(*b*) Those already landed had taken up a position whence they could protect the landing ground and prevent removal of the sign.

Immediately he decided to send out a small party of No. 1 Section to the rough cover at B, from which their fire could sweep the landing ground from end to end.

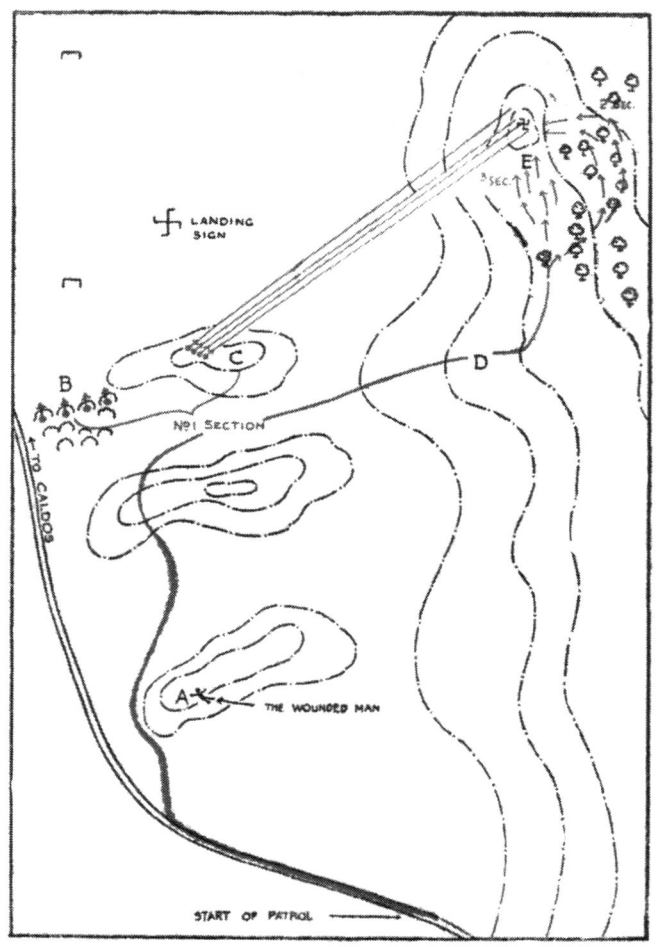

PLATE 4

He then sent the rest of No. 1 Section forward to give covering fire from the hill at C and ordered Nos. 2 and 3 Sections to climb the hill in the dead ground at D which the enemy could not cover from their position at E, and then to split into separate sections, attacking both flanks of the enemy from the rear.

The operation was well synchronized and the covering party did not open fire till Nos. 2 and 3 Sections had had time to get into position for the final assault. Then they opened rapid fire. The attacking sections were defiladed from the covering fire by the brow of the hill and pounced upon the enemy before they could take their attention off the covering party, which furnished an admirable distraction and ceased fire as soon as the yells of the attackers were heard.

Immediately after scuppering this party, and before their bayonets were dry, the Leader got the whole patrol dispersed to cover the landing ground, leaving the landing sign to draw more enemy into the trap.

That's the stuff to give them!

And now, before I finish, let me give you two final hints. Vital ones. If you aspire to be a Fighting Patrol Leader master these two points and you will be a good one.

FIRST. This is how nearly all fighting patrols fail, if they fail at all. They DISSIPATE their force.

Suppose there are fifteen Germans acting in a body and a fighting patrol twenty-five strong is after them. They should be easy meat, but ONLY IF THE **fighting patrol keeps together.**

If the Patrol Leader splits his forces up into three sections and lets them go into the blue working more or less independently, one consisting of eight men will bump into the fifteen Boches and get the worst of it. Then along will come another section of eight and meet the same fate, but if the whole lot had kept together and one section had smitten the enemy with covering fire whilst the other two charged their flanks, the fifteen would have had no chance at all.

This seems almost self-evident, but you will see how everything will conspire to induce you to spread out your forces when you go on patrol. You will set out as a compact body, but in a few hundred yards your men will be straggled all over the place. Make up your mind inflexibly that except for the scouts you are going to keep all your men in a compact body so that you can use them all together to hit the enemy a strong, forceful and heavy blow.

The SECOND great failing is that the patrol LOSES ITS MOMENTUM. It sets off in great style, full of fire and fury. Then a distant shot is heard and immediately everyone in the patrol starts creeping, crawling, taking cover and returning the fire. This is just what the Germans want: they can take careful, steady aim, they can pick the patrol off one by one, they can carry out their plans unhindered, and they feel on TOP.

But how different their feelings when they open fire on a patrol which, instead of faltering or hesitating, shows determination to come to grips, a patrol which firmly and resolutely carries out a dashing attack, every man knowing exactly what is required of him!

Then the Germans' fire becomes wild and inaccurate. They begin to think about their retreat. They glance with fear at the glinting bayonets which begin to converge. Their stomachs turn to ice. They sense the deadly determination of the approaching patrol, and before they know it, without any orders from their brains, their legs are running like hell.

This concludes my sketch outline of fighting patrols. You have the framework: let your own exercise and experience fill in the gaps.

And then, when the Great Moment comes for you to lead your fighting patrol against the invading Huns KEEP YOUR MEN TOGETHER, KEEP UP YOUR MOMENTUM, and you will find yourself enjoying the FINEST SPORT ON EARTH!

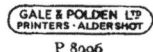

P 8996

www.ingramcontent.com/pod-product-compliance
Ingram Content Group UK Ltd.
Pitfield, Milton Keynes, MK11 3LW, UK
UKHW042000230426
12048UKWH00009B/441